Money Loves Attention

Lessons on Financial Freedom and How to Avoid a Toxic Relationship with Money

PATRICK A HOWARD, MBA

BEST SELLING BOOKS PUBLISHED BY HOWARD GLOBAL ENTERPRISE

by Rainie Howard

ADDICTED TO PAIN
Renew Your Mind and Heal Your Spirit
From A Toxic Relationship in 30 Day

YOU ARE ENOUGH
Overcoming People Pleasing and
Emotionally Unavailable Relationships

WHEN GOD SENT MY HUSBAND
Wisdoms for Capturing and Keeping a Man's Heart

UNDENIABLE BREAKTHROUGH
Spiritual Guide and Life Journal

MIRACLES IN YOUR MOUTH
Be Renewed, Overcome Anxiety, Fear and Depression
Through Spiritual Principles & Life-Changing Affirmations

By Patrick and Rainie Howard

DECIDING TO LOVE
Turn Your Argumentative, Frustrating, Painful Relationship Into An Understanding, Healthy, Happy, Loving Relationship

Howard Global Enterprises Publishing Agency

Scripture quotations are taken from the Holy Bible. All rights reserved worldwide.

Copyright © 2021 Howard Global Enterprises

All rights reserved, including the right to reproduce this book or portions thereof in any form whatsoever. No part of this production may be reproduced or transmitted in any form or by any means, mechanical or electronic, including photocopying or recording, or by any information storage and retrieval system, or transmitted by email without permission in writing form the publisher. While all attempts have been made to verify the information provided in this publication, neither the author nor the publisher assumes any responsibility for errors, omissions, or contrary interpretations of the subject matter herein. The views expressed are those of the author, and should not be taken as legal, financial or other professional advice. The reader is responsible for his or her own actions. Neither the author nor the publisher assumes any responsibility or liability whatsoever on the behalf of the purchaser or reader of these materials. Any perceived slight of any individual or organization is purely unintentional.

Published by Howard Global Enterprises LLC

Howard Global Enterprises LLC
2404 Centerline Industrial Drive
Maryland Heights, MO

For information contact Howard Global Enterprises, LLC at www.moneylovesattention.com

For information about special discounts for bulk purchases or bringing the author to your live event, please contact Howard Global Enterprises Sales at 314-827-5216 or cfo@realloveexist.com

Manufactured in the United State of America

ISBN: 978-1-7365203-0-7

ACKNOWLEDGEMENTS

I would like to acknowledge and thank my wonderful and amazing wife, Rainie Howard. You are a true inspiration and I wouldn't have completed this book without your love and support. I love you so much. Special thanks to my children, Patrick B. and Aniyah. You kids inspire me in ways you can't even understand. I am such a proud father and truly blessed by both of you.

Lastly, special thanks to all of my mentors both past and present. The lessons I have learned from each of you have been a great contributor to my life.

TABLE OF CONTENTS

INTRODUCTION 9

CHAPTER 1: HOW YOU LEARN ABOUT MONEY MATTERS 15

CHAPTER 2: DATE YOUR MONEY 25

CHAPTER 3: FACE IT TIL' YOU MAKE IT 33

CHAPTER 4: WEALTH IS HEALTH 45

CHAPTER 5: MONEY BLOCKS AND HOW THEY LOWER YOUR STANDARDS 53

CHAPTER 6: YOUR SOURCE HAS UNLIMITED RESOURCES 63

CHAPTER 7: VICTIMS, CONSUMERS, OR PRODUCERS 71

CHAPTER 8: NET WORTH DOES NOT EQUAL SELF WORTH 83

CHAPTER 9: GIVING, RECEIVING & GRATITUDE 97

CONCLUSION 107

AFFIRMATIONS 109

BUDGET TEMPLATE EXAMPLE 113

ABOUT THE AUTHOR 115

INTRODUCTION

As a finance professional and tax consultant, I have spent the majority of my adult life studying money theories and money management principles. As an undergraduate, I earned a bachelor's degree in accounting from Chicago State University in Chicago Illinois and an MBA from Webster University in St. Louis Missouri. Following my education and throughout my personal and professional experience as a tax and finance consultant, I have identified key concepts of financial freedom that lead me to the title, ideas, and desire to write this book.

As a finance consultant in public and private enterprises, I have serviced large and mid-sized corporations and individual clients, ranging from millionaire executives, professional athletes, small business owners to the common family working to make ends meet. In my experience, I noticed that regardless of the level of life my clients were experiencing or the decisions that needed to be made, both personal and professional, all clients have one thing in common: money controls how they make non-financial and financial decisions. I understand that my clients come to me for money management strategies and advice, so the fact that decisions are based around money is expected. However, I have notice that most actions after our discussions are not always made based on whether the client has enough money or not, but rather on their belief system surrounding money and their relationship with money.

Money is a tool. A definition of money is the means we use to make payment in exchange for something desired. Often people forget that money is a tool and create an unhealthy reliance and relationship with money. People put their trust in money, serve money, and are controlled by the thought of gaining and losing money. As a result of these traits, people spend a lot of time worrying about money, adore money, and take offense when talking about money. Operating like this can cause toxic relationships and the acceptance of toxic behavior all because money is involved.

My wife and I have published several books together surrounding the topic of relationships. The first book we wrote is titled, "When God Sent My Husband." This book mostly explores a single woman's journey in preparing herself to be ready for a committed relationship and ultimately getting married. It gets to the root of her belief system which needed to be addressed and adjusted to receive the best of what God has for her in a husband. Our second book together is titled, "Deciding to Love." This book addresses how to address and overcome challenges in a relationship. This book goes in detail on how one's thoughts control actions and how this impacts their interaction with the person they are in a relationship with.

When I decided I wanted to write a book about money, I took the idea to my writing consultant and partner, my wife. When we were discussing the topics of this book and reflected on how people's thought patterns surrounding money are distorted, it reminded us of how people deal with other individuals in relationships. Just as in the books we wrote about personal relationships, our discussion on the topic of money reminded us that many people aren't adequately prepared to manage money and are not equipped to handle the change and challenge of money management.

Then the thought arose, if money was a person (in theory), what would that relationship look like. Would it be healthy, or would it be toxic? In addition, what are the key drivers causing relationships to be the way that they are. Ultimately, one's relationship with money is a direct reflection of that person's thoughts and experiences, just like they are in person to person relationships. So, the question to ask is, "what thoughts are controlling people's relationship with money?"

The Bible teaches that "as a man thinks within himself, so he is." Thus, it is key to understand that in order to change your outer world, one must first renew their mind and change their inner thoughts and perceptions of money. Often, the baggage of one's past is the key contributor to how they view money and their interaction with it throughout their lives.

Money Loves Attention will expose the mindsets that hold people back and will inspire you to identify and overcome money traumas, break incorrect generational mindsets concerning money, and help you learn the laws of money that generate financial freedom. Some of the topics discussed in the chapters to follow may seem trivial or superficial; but the truth is, many ideas concerning money are not as complicated as you may believe. The attraction of money is connected to what people believe. There are moments in life when it may seem that the only way to truly understand money management is by hiring a financial expert, like me, but some of the most basic strategies reveal themselves when you change your thinking and beliefs about money. Therefore, I challenge you to read this book in its entirety and implement the action plans and affirmations given to reprogram how you view money and thereby create financial freedom in your life.

CHAPTER 1

HOW YOU LEARN ABOUT MONEY MATTERS

One of the biggest contributors to how we learn about money is our upbringing. Many of our money philosophies about spending habits, savings, and investment strategies all stem from what we had observed as children - whether it was seeing your parents cut costs to make ends meet or they spent money frivolously on things they desired. They could have kept large sums of cash to make purchases or used credit cards. Whatever the case, our first teachers about money management were our parents and the people close to us. Most of the time, they gave us unintentional lessons, but they had a major impact on how we now act as adults and even on the way we teach our kids about money.

When I was fourteen and a half years old, my stepfather insisted I learn to drive. He would say, "Pat, it's important you learn to drive because you never want to depend on anyone to take you home when you are ready to leave a place." He would further explain, "You should be in complete control of where you are, how long you stay and whether or not you leave. For example, if you were to go to a party and wanted to leave, you could just leave. You wouldn't have to ask or wait on anyone." The logic in which he explained my necessity to learn to drive made sense and I was eager to learn.

Right before my 15th birthday, he purchased a car for me. It was a navy blue 1990 Nissan Stanza. To keep from making a big deal out of the purchase, he claimed it was a cheap learning car that only costed $1,000. On several different occasions, he would remind others who asked about the car that it was a cheap car at $1000. One thousand dollars was an amazing deal for a nicely kept running car with a sunroof, in my mind. Nevertheless, he made a point of stating, "It was $1000 and if it broke down or something, we could just get another one at that price easily."

I only drove the car a few times, because the car broke down within months of having it and could not be repaired. However, just as he had stated, we were able to look in the newspaper (this was before Craigslist and internet shopping) and found another car for the same price. It was a light blue

Pontiac Grand Am with a slight oil leak but otherwise still drove well. We met up with the owner, checked out the car and just as easily as the first one, I had another car a few months before my 16th birthday.

From this experience as a teenager, I learned three lessons: cheap cars should be the first option when learning to drive; second, cheap cars are easy to find; and last, always seek to control your environment if possible.

This is a subtle example of how a parent's well-meaning gestures can become life lessons for an adolescent. Our experiences educate us and provide a level of expectations for how easy or challenging it might be to obtain the things we desire. It also gives us an idea of how much control we have over our circumstances.

For example, have you ever been told you couldn't get that new pair of shoes because they are too expensive? Have you ever been told you couldn't get that new shirt because you didn't need it? Have you ever been told to pick a food item that costs less than what you originally wanted? What did this teach you? The subliminal message here is that some things are in fact expensive, not easy to obtain, and in some cases not even worth the value, and not necessary to desire, because they can easily be substituted with something cheaper.

Have you ever considered the impact this could have on your current perception on your usage of money and what you deem expensive or necessary? Many people take their past experiences and apply them to their current life. These past experiences determine if a person makes decisions from an abundance mindset or a poverty mindset. An abundance mindset is the belief there is more than enough of everything (including money) for everyone. A poverty mindset is the belief that things are hard to get, money is hard to earn, and there aren't enough resources for everyone. I'll talk about these two mindsets later in the book, but they are very important to how you live your life.

For example, if you grow up in a household where your parents discuss the expensive bills and stress over the over usage of utilities, when you become an adult, most likely you will do the same thing. The impact could have two effects: it could cause someone to underutilize utilities, even if they can afford the bill either way, or it could cause someone to overcompensate, holding the notion, "When I was young, my parents couldn't afford it, so I'm doing what I could never do - to the max." Whatever your ultimate approach, these two outlooks are rooted in your past experiences. If we stay too focused on the past and drag those experiences into the present, we risk recreating those past feelings in the current moment. If you grew up with a fear of lack, you might possibly create those same feelings, even if you are not in the same state financially.

This is why it is important to renew your mindset through prayer, meditation and affirmations. The Bible teaches the importance of renewing your mind as the key to sharpening your discernment to help you make better life decisions. People are commonly controlled by how they were raised, what they see on the news, and what their peer group experiences. Thus, we must create a routine of habits that include prayer, meditation, and affirmations to reprogram our thinking. The goal of reprograming through routine is not to overlook your past but to identify the sources of your thinking, add new meaning to those experiences, and make those moments more empowering as you move forward in your economic future.

As for my experience with my stepfather and the lessons I learned from the car purchase, it seems logical that they ultimately created money blocks in my early adult life. What exactly are money blocks? Money blocks are negative subconscious beliefs about money that limit you from achieving your conscious desires. For example, because I thought first cars should be cheap, when it came time to make financial decisions, my first thought was look for the cheaper option. I didn't consider reliability, value or purpose, just cheap. In addition to cheap, if the item being purchased broke or needed to be replaced, no worry because cheap deals saved me money and bargains for replacement and or repair are easy to find.

Operating with such ideals gives the impression of control over spending and the environment. However, to the contrary, cheap in some instances meant sacrificing quality and reliability. And though it seemed that I was controlling my spending by seeking the cheaper option first, the replacement cost for these items exceeded the initial price of a more reliable and quality purchase, and it cost me more money in the long term.

For this reason, I was required to reprogram my thinking related to the many lessons learned as a youth. If you have experienced any situation, had any recommendation, or observed scarcity behavior, know that you are not captive to operating with the same philosophy and mindset. You have the power to reprogram your perspective and create the life you desire, without the limitations of your past caused by past generations.

STATEMENT OF AFFIRMATION

——————— ❧❦❧ ———————

I have overcome the challenges of my past and I am positioned for greatness in my future. I possess the skills and abilities to achieve God's purpose for my future. I am committed to the actions necessary to create the life I desire. I am thankful for all I have and the blessings to come in my life. I am healthy, wealthy, and my life is filled with joy.

ACTION PLAN

——————— ❧❦❧ ———————

Just as athletes have to practice to prepare their mind for game situations, so should we practice preparing our minds for life's situations. Therefore, commit to settings aside 15 minutes daily for prayer, meditation and affirmations to renew your mind. Remember that your thoughts will manifest in your life, so take this time to address the things that have been holding you back and elevate your thinking to becoming a person fit to fulfill your purpose.

"You have the power to reprogram your perspective and create the life you desire, without the limitations of your past or past generations."

CHAPTER 2

DATE YOUR MONEY

When my wife and I were dating, we would talk for long hours over the phone about our dreams, future goals and vision for our lives. We had fun every time we hung out. We enjoyed talking about what we had going on while dreaming of what our future would look like. While hanging out, talking and having fun with each other, we were able to identify how our values connected and that we were a great complement for each other. The more we hung out and communicated with each other, the closer we grew.

There was a moment during our courtship when we were required to have a long-distance relationship. During this time, we both had individual schedules and obligations, but we were certain to make time to talk to each other. Whether it was a "How's your day?" evening update or an update on the week, we made an effort to check in on each other to affirm that we were thinking about each other. Though physical distance created a challenging time for our relationship, the fact that we continued to communicate and check in helped us stay connected while we were physically apart. Ultimately, our commitment to each other, rooted on the remembrance of our shared love, goals, and how much we enjoyed each other's presence helped us overcome this challenging season in our relationship.

When the opportunity presented itself to reconnect in the same place, I took advantage of it and relocated. However, once we were reconnected in the same city, I was distracted by other commitments and the newness of life in a different city. I lost focus on dating and spending time and my attention was wrapped up in other things aside from our relationship. As a result, our relationship became stagnant.

When it comes to money, people often start in the same place as they do in relationships, that is, with nothing except dreams, goals and visions. Most people don't have large sums of money to start their adult lives, nor have they been taught financial principles on how to manage or grow money after it has been acquired. Prior to having money, they can only imagine themselves with money and enjoying life to the best of their experiences and expectations. And the best of most people expectations is often based on the mindset of their environment and entertainment. This is the reason why renewing one's mindset is a major key to overcoming generational and societal norms and thought patterns.

Yet, many of us have jobs, careers, families and other obligations; and though money is a major source in these activities, many fail to check in on their financial health when they start receiving money more frequently. Goals can easily be replaced with the desire to only earn "good" money and the steps needed to accomplishing goals are replaced with money traumas from past experiences that dictate how goals are viewed and pursued.

At times, it can be easy to get distracted by life obligations and become complacent and stagnant in your relationship with money and pursuing your life goals. As a result, many people are unaware that they are so consumed with the use of money that they are not connected with the flow of money in their life. Even when individuals make more money or when money is more available and present, they still overlook the importance of checking the pulse of their financial health. For this reason, it is necessary to plan dates with your money to ensure you understand its flow. Dates with your money can help you identify how to maximize your earning potential and maintain a stable financial health.

What does a money date look like? Here are steps to having a successful money date.

Step 1. Set a date each month when you will look over your money. Plan to look beyond your current cash balance in the bank. Look at how your money is earned and spent to determine any habits needing adjustment.

Step 2. Make a budget. Budgets are basically plans for how you spend your money. Most people put more focus on the making the budget plan than implementing it. Therefore, don't let creating a budget keep you from implementing a budget plan or financial strategy. (Note: If you are in need of a budget template, I provide one at the end of this book.)

Step 3. Upon evaluation of your performance, when reviewing your finances, celebrate the wins. It's not enough to work and pay bills, but you should also have fun with the money you earn. Remember to treat yourself each month to something you enjoy. Just as in relationships with people, doing things you enjoy makes for a more happy and healthy relationship with money.

STATEMENT OF AFFIRMATION

I am a great manager of my money. Money comes to me in expected and unexpected ways. I attract more money into my life by thinking of the things I desire to accomplish. I have more than enough and everything I need to accomplish my goals. I have clear goals, and I will never stop trying until I have accomplished all I desire. I am healthy, wealthy, and my life is filled with joy.

ACTION PLAN

While preparing for your money date, ask yourself:

Question: Are you happy with the way things are and are you enjoying your money?

If you don't like where you work or feel overworked and underpaid, this could impact your relationship with money.

Question: Does something need to change for you to enjoy your money? Are you feeling desperate for money?

Remember, just as in finding a mate, as it relate to money, you should never be desperate. Desperation for money can cause the acceptance of toxic behavior concerning money and create toxic unhealthy and unjoyful experiences surrounding money.

Question: What do you want to do with your money?

Recognize that accomplishing goals may take time, but it does not matter how long it takes as long as you don't stop pursuing them. Thus, if your life goals don't match your cash flow, be willing to make the necessary changes to further your pursuit of your goals and create the income you desire to do the things you enjoy.

"Make dates with your money to ensure you understand the flow of your money, you can identify how to maximize your earning potential and maintain stable financial health."

CHAPTER 3

FACE IT TIL' YOU MAKE IT

Napoleon Hill (author of Think and Grow Rich), during an interview with Andrew Carnegie asked, why were some wage-earning people not as rich as Carnegie though they felt they were working to the best of their ability? Per the interview, Carnegie answered by explaining the law of compensation. In summary, the law of compensation is that people earn income based on what they expect from what they do. In addition, one's earnings are tied directly to what they have done in the past to prepare for their current compensation.

Many people don't understand this law, nor do they have clear expectations of what their compensation should be. Not knowing the value of your work limits your earning potential to the value someone else has placed on your contribution. For this reason, you see many people with college degrees earning well below their earning potential. On the other side of the coin, you see new college graduates with false expectations for their salaries with no work experience to warrant the desired pay scale. Though pay scales can be easily researched, they are often disregarded as a means for determining the actual worth of one's expertise. Pay scales vary based on company size, location and the willingness to pay for services rendered.

Early in my career as a finance consultant, I met many different people, but two types stuck out. The first is the "fake it until you make it" person. Their goal is to act confident and successful to convince others they had accomplished what they sought professionally, that is, to influence others to support them financially to eventually accomplishing their goals.

The outward appearance of this person is creating a belief system that ultimately manifests in their life monetarily. However, in private, many complain of feeling defeated, struggling, and having no support or anyone to turn to. In addition, they often question their ability to keep the act up over the long haul and don't have a clue what they should do next if their current plans don't work out. It is a bit of a contradiction to how they are in public. Their actions don't match their belief system.

The other type is all about actions. They don't care about acclaim or recognition but are more attached to the purpose, vision and impact of their actions and business ventures. This person knows that it doesn't matter how well they are known if it didn't translate into acquiring the necessary resources to fulfill their vision. They understand that accomplishing their plans requires resources and they are relentless in doing whatever is necessary to acquire the resources to carry out their vision and maximize what they believe their impact should be.

In comparing the two personality types, the difference boils down to mindset and an understanding of the law of compensation. One understands that life now is but a reflection of what you believe, combined with the actions you take (based on those beliefs) and the value you add. The other believes that regardless of their beliefs, if they can convince others to believe in their success, it will generate what they desire financially.

What are your beliefs? Do you plan to fake it until you make it, or do you plan to face your challenges directly and overcome them realistically? The key is to know the level you want to be on and contribute at the level. Understand that if your goal is to be promoted, you should already be performing at that level. Don't wait until you get an opportunity to be a CEO. See your life as a system where you are already the CEO and operate in a manner that complements where you are. This is a key contributor to where you want to be in the future. It all starts with your mind and what you believe. Recognize that what you do today will pay dividends in the future, so you cannot take lightly the work you currently do.

As the Bible teaches, despise not small beginnings. Be a good steward over the little you have and prepare yourself (mentally) to be a good steward of more. Never allow the feelings of others to control what you believe about yourself. Regardless of how others feel, it is important that you believe you are fully equipped to be the person you desire to be. In addition, take control of your life by not allowing yourself to be moved by too much praise or criticism. If you believe you are who you need to be and operate in that manner, the things you are believing for will manifest in your physical life. Your actions are a direct reflection of what you believe more than your words and what others believe.

STORY OF FAITH IN ACTION

After celebrating my one-year anniversary as a senior tax accountant and receiving great reviews on my annual evaluation, I felt perfectly positioned for a promotion. I had my eyes set on becoming the next tax manager for U.S. operations. Soon after these evaluations, I was requested to join a newly created mentor program for high performers. I was matched with the Vice President and General Counsel, who was second in command to the CEO. My manager was the CFO of North America operations, so this matching seemed like a great fit and preparation for where I thought I was headed.

After a year of meeting with my mentor, setting goals, and completing activities, while at the same time maintaining a high level of work performance, I thought for sure that I would be promoted. I met with the CFO for my annual review and again received a great evaluation, just as the year before. Also, like the year before, it was communicated that although I had accomplished so much, I had still not received the promotion hoped for. At this point, I was a bit perturbed, but I held onto my faith that God would open the door for me if I stayed faithful and diligent with what I had.

In addition to my faith, I knew the importance of writing my vision down, looking at it daily, and being willing to do the work to fulfill my vision. So, the next thing I did was print my name and the title I desired: Tax Manager. I hung it up on my cubicle wall to view every day. This was a daily reminder of where I saw myself and also of the work needed from me. I needed to operate as if I were already the manager on my way to becoming it officially, and the name and titled printed on the wall was my reminder of this.

I also researched pay scales and determined the exact salary I desired. I wrote the salary down on a small piece of paper, folded it up, and placed it in my wallet. From that moment forward, I was determined to operate in such a manner that would manifest the role and desires I had for a career promotion.

Whenever my co-workers would pass my cubicle and see my name and title as manager printed on paper on the wall, knowing that I wasn't officially the manager, they laughed at seeing it. Some would mock my posting and jokingly say, "I'm the manager too." They didn't understand why I posted it, nor did I feel the need to explain it. I stayed focused on my vision and didn't allow their doubts or criticism to cause me to doubt myself. I understood the law of compensation, and I was clear about where I saw myself based on the contribution I was making to the company.

Thus, whenever there was an opportunity to contribute on a higher level, I took the chance. If someone needed support on a project, I volunteered to assist. And when financial analysis was needed, I took the approach of considering what information would be most useful to the CFO and what could be done to create the biggest benefit to the organization.

After six months of operating with such faith, reminders, and effort, I was called into my manager's office. My efforts had finally paid off, and I was offered the exact title I had hanging in my cubicle. At this time, I was informed that I would also be receiving a salary increase as part of the promotion to match the title change. I was given the promotion documents with the title change along with the salary increase. When I got back to my desk, I compared the salary I had written down to the salary increase I had received; the salary I received was much smaller than the amount I wrote down. I was grateful for the promotion, but only partially fulfilled because I knew my value was much higher than the increase. Nevertheless, I continued to press on with the same work ethic to prove that I was capable of more and much more valuable.

To my surprise, three months later I was requested to come to a meeting with my manager. I was informed that one of the senior managers had decided to resign and I was offered their job. If I was willing to take on the job, it would come with another title change and an additional salary increase. Considering my goal at the beginning of the year was to be promoted and increase my salary, I accepted the opportunity. When I was given the new promotion documentation and salary increase, I noticed that the salary I had written down exactly matched the increase received.

I believe that because I had a clear vision of where I wanted to be, along with the willingness to do what it took to get there, God knew the exact doors to open to provide the opportunity to fulfill my vision. Not every situation in life will happen as quickly as mine did, but I am a firm believer that we have the power to create the future we desire when we match our faith with our actions. You may never know how an opportunity will present itself, so in pursuit of your goals, keep an open mind and be willing to adapt to the changes needed and keep moving closer to your goals.

Never allow your present moment or the doubt of others to deter you from the work required to progress to your destiny. It might not happen right away, and the people around you may not understand your faith and even laugh or mock your process, but keep your faith that God will bring you closer to the desires of your heart daily. Just be sure your actions match what you believe. Your faith will be challenged along the way, but face your present moments with courage and create the feelings now for the future you desire.

STATEMENT OF AFFIRMATION

———————— ⁕⁓⁕ ————————

I am so happy and thankful, now that I have the ability to create the future life I desire. I am faithful and diligent in managing everything God has called me to manage. Every day, I do my best and I trust God for the outcome. I am healthy, wealthy, and my life is filled with joy.

ACTION PLAN

———————— ⁕⁓⁕ ————————

What do you desire? Write it down. After you know what you desire, set 1-3 tasks to complete each day to help you move closer to those desires. If you don't have clear professional goals, set your mind on accomplishing personal goals and completing self-improvement tasks. You can watch YouTube videos or read something that helps you improve your mind. Do something that brings you joy and uplifts your spirit. Work on becoming the best version of yourself by doing the inner work and using your time to contribute to your growth each day. Remind yourself that what you do now will pay dividends in the future.

"Never allow your present moment or the doubt of others to deter you from doing the work required of you to progress to your destiny."

CHAPTER 4

―――― ❧☙❧☙ ――――

WEALTH IS HEALTH

"HEALTH IS LIKE MONEY. WE NEVER HAVE A TRUE IDEA OF ITS VALUE UNTIL WE LOSE IT."
JOSH BILLINGS

As a young adult, you feel invincible. It would be no big deal to stay up late watching TV or working and eating unhealthy foods, drinks and snacks. As one ages, they quickly realize that staying up late and eating unhealthily are damaging to overall well-being. This is a lesson that many people learn too late in life. The problem with learning this lesson too late in life is that in doing so, one sacrifices their ability to potentially enjoy life at an older age.

Early in my career, I was a mid-level accountant, working my way up the corporate ladder for an aerospace company. At the time, my wife and I had been married for a few years and our children were 2 and 3. In my aspirations to continue to grow in my career and increase my earning potential, I decided that I wanted and needed to attend graduate school to earn a Master's in Business Administration (MBA). My plan was to work in the day, spend time with my family in the evenings, and do my graduate studies at night. Considering that I was in my early twenties, I thought it would be no problem to do this and be successful.

I would soon learn how daunting this task would be on a daily basis as there was never enough time in the day to do everything. There were evenings when I would come home from work between 6:30pm and 7:30pm and try to dedicate my time to my family from the time I was home until the kids' bedtime - roughly 8:30pm to 9pm. Then I would spend a little couples time with my wife until she was tired which was roughly around 11pm or 11:30pm. After that, I would focus on my graduate studies for my MBA. At times, this would last until 3:00am to 4:00am. I wasn't always the most alert during this time, but candy was my go-to snack to keep me up, alert and awake in getting the work done. I figured that as long as I could get work done and get to bed by 4:00am, three hours of sleep was sufficient enough to get to work by 8:30am and be rested enough for the day.

After close to a year of operating with such an extensive schedule, where I sacrificed sleep, working out and healthy eating, I started to experience light headaches and stomach pains. I didn't think much of it and attributed it to a lack of sleep. I figured that if I could catch up on my sleep on weekends, I would be fine. After trying to catch up on my sleep over the weekend, my headaches went away but my stomach issues persisted. I had always been healthy and athletic as a former collegiate baseball player, so I was accustomed to some discomfort; but when my stomach pains persisted even to the light touch, I could no longer take the pain and decided to visit a doctor for a checkup.

After a visit to the doctor, it was identified that my stomach pains were the result of ulcers. All the stress of career, family, and school that I had been putting on myself caused peptic ulcers in my stomach. I was immediately put on a diet, given an antibiotic regimen of pills and was recommended to reduce my stress levels and get more rest. I immediately was reminded that though I was driven and focused on doing all I needed to do to further my career and earning potential, it was important not to sacrifice my health in the process. Prior to this moment, I took pride in professional recognition and success.

But, in the face of health concerns, I soon realized that those things were meaningless if I didn't possess the health to enjoy them.

The lesson in this is to take care of yourself. It can be easy to become overworked, overconsumed and stressed by your obligations and aspirations of increasing your income and creating the life of your dreams. It is important to be willing to do the work to accomplish the goals we desire, but it is equally important that we take care of ourselves in the process. Don't allow yourself to be mistreated by others or yourself for the sake of earning money.

It can be easy to spot when someone is taking advantage of you but not as easy to identify when we mistreat ourselves for the sake of money. It is important to acknowledge that we have the freedom to decide what we are willing to do to maintain and or increase our earning potential. At the same time, we must recognize that we can maximize our impact when we are the best version of ourselves in mind, body and spirit. We should never sacrifice any of these three elements for the sake of earning money. The body is your temple, and your temple requires regular maintenance and attention. Therefore, get your rest, eat healthy, and exercise. It will serve you in being your best self while earning income and enjoying the fruits of your labor.

STATEMENT OF AFFIRMATION

I am so happy and thankful now that my life is filled with great health. I am the master of my life, and money serves me for the benefit of my health, joy and fulfilling my purpose. My health is top priority in my life, and I am so happy and thankful that I have a healthy mind, body and spirit.

ACTION PLAN

When managing a busy schedule, it is key to take breaks and schedule some "me time." Remember that personal time is a benefit to take advantage of regularly, even when you don't have an elaborate vacation or special event planned. After completing daunting and challenging tasks, schedule time for a vacation or "staycation" to renew your mind, body and spirit to endure. Create healthy eating habits and sleep patterns and be sure you are the number one priority. Just as a corporation looks at profits as its bottom line, you should also consider what profit there is in gaining all the wealth you desire but lose the health and strength to enjoy it.

MONEY LOVES ATTENTION

"Don't allow yourself to be mistreated by others or yourself for the sake of earning money."

CHAPTER 5

MONEY BLOCKS AND HOW THEY LOWER YOUR STANDARDS

Life is filled with pivotal moments where decisions are made whether to hold tight to your dreams/visions or lower your standards. The key to taking control of your life is being clear when concessions need to be made to acclimate to your reality. However, never compromise on your standards. Effectively adjusting to the different seasons of life may require give and take and some flexibility to keep moving forward to accomplish your goals and live out your vision. Nevertheless, it is important while maintaining flexibility to never discount or lower your standards to fit the external environment. Doing so will ultimately result in potentially blocking your blessings. Discounting and/or lowering your standards will take you off the path of achieving your goals and put you in a state of apathy.

Early in the book, I brought up money blocks. As a reminder, money blocks are negative subconscious beliefs that limit you from achieving your desires. Money blocks can lead to having a scarcity mindset. Money blocks are the reason why so many people are stuck in the same economic place year after year whether they wish to progress or not. I will touch on some of the most common money blocks that hold people back in hopes that as they are exposed, they can be overcame.

Money Block #1: "More money, More problems."

Growing up in the 90's, one of the biggest songs of the era was by Puff Daddy (P. Diddy) and the Family titled, "Mo Money, Mo Problems." The song was loosely based on the success of Bad Boy Records and the life of Notorious BIG. The title expressed the feelings that the more successful they were the more haters and problems they encountered. This is a common belief in the popular culture but having such a belief can do two things: either it pushes money away or it manifests problems as one's money increases.

As a result, people can subconsciously self-sabotage their growth based on the fear of problems that come with gaining wealth or becoming rich. In an effort to avoid such problems, statements such as, "I don't want to be rich or I am content with where I am" guide people toward a life of lack or just enough when, though in fact, they have the potential to earn more.

Money Block #2: "I Can't Afford It."

Have you ever looked at the price of an item and said, "I can't afford it?" Repeating this statement creates a block to experiencing the life you desire. Most people don't have a budget and or tracking system for their money to know what they should and should not purchase at any given time. Most purchases are based on impulse and the desire to fill a void inside. At the end of the day, people make purchases based on what they value and not on what they have calculated they can spend or afford.

There is a saying, "people buy what they want, not what they need." Thus, you should never say, "I can't afford it." If an item's cost extends beyond what you are willing to pay or what your bank account allows, just state that it is not what you are interested in doing at this time and not that you can't afford it. In cases where it is not a wise decision to make certain purchases, state that you do not desire to make the purchase. You should also avoid saying that you can't afford something because it can create negative feelings towards things and also impact one's willingness to work for them. Considering the fact that most people buy what they want, when one communicates to their family that they can't afford something, the family could feel that their wants or desires are not important. This is because of a belief that if you are willing to pay for something, especially if you are tight on money, it must be important.

Money Block #3: "Money Doesn't Grow on Trees / Money is Hard to Make"

This is a message learned early in life, but it often sticks with people well into their adult years. The idea that money doesn't grow on trees affirms the scarcity mindset that money is hard to make and not easy to get. If I could only grow a money tree and take from it whenever I need a dollar, then I would always have what I want. This is coupled with the idea that earning money takes lots of time and hard work. Thus, the harder you work, the more money you can receive over time.

This mentality creates roadblocks to promotions, and thoughts of feeling unworthy.

Recognize that you are worthy to receive all that God has planned for you and that nothing is too hard or too good for you to receive. Money isn't hard to make; it is easy to make but requires skill to keep. Nevertheless, you were born with everything you need to make money easily, and you are worthy of anything you desire right now.

These three money blocks keep people in a state of scarcity and are major contributors in widening the wealth gap. The reason this is taking place has nothing to do with the lack of opportunities, but the generational mindsets passed down in families. These blocks and mindsets are passed down rooted in fear. Fear of failure is often talked about as motivation that keeps people from giving up, but there also exists a fear of success that can have the opposite effect.

This is connected directly with the mindset of more money, more problems, but not all problems are bad. In addition, government policies and tax incentives have focused on the lower middle and lower classes, thus creating a dependent social culture that in some instances would prefer to remain in a specific income range to receive those incentives.

I have worked with many clients who have seen success in their careers with increased income; and as a result, they were required to pay more tax than they had in the past. Some clients accepted this change. For these clients, we discuss tax savings strategies and consider making additional estimated tax payments to be sure their tax obligation is fulfilled with the least amount due come tax time in April.

Other clients don't accept the change or make any adjustments. They would complain that though it seemed that their income had increased, it wasn't by enough to afford the additional tax. Some were upset that tax credits had started to phase out due to their income level. Some were no longer eligible for credits such as the earned income tax credit they were accustomed to getting year after year. Due to all these changes, there were even moments when they questioned if I miscalculated their returns to avoid the higher tax expense.

Lastly, if they didn't qualify for any additional credits, they would even ask me what they could do to lower their income.

The issue with this is that the tax code is written to benefit those with businesses, but individuals who are employees have the least incentives to lower income for tax purposes. In addition, credits such as the earned income tax credit and stimulus checks are reserved to benefit working people with a low to moderate income. Thus, once someone exceeds what is considered a moderate income, they are no longer eligible for certain tax incentives.

Because of this added problem, some people would rather remain in the low to moderate income range just to be eligible for benefits. I conducted a small survey to ask low to moderate income individuals if they desired to be rich, and as much as I would like to say that everyone said, yes, not all did. Some responded that they had no desire to be rich and were content with where they were even though by government standards they needed financial assistance.

This is the reason why you should address money blocks as soon as they are identified. If you don't, they will do nothing but create a mindset that deceives you into thinking you are being thoughtful when, actually, you are operating in fear and scarcity.

STATEMENT OF AFFIRMATION

I am so happy and thankful now that I have overcome my past thoughts. I have put on the mind of God, and my life is filled with abundance in every area. I am worthy of all the desires of my heart, and I am wealthy and can afford anything I desire. I am healthy, wealthy, and my life is filled with joy.

ACTION PLAN

A positive mind is the best defense against money blocks. Affirmations play a key role in reprograming your mind to no longer allow money blocks to control your thinking. Thus, it is important to remind yourself of the affirmation above every morning and night. Record yourself saying the affirmations to reinforce the thought that you are wealthy, healthy and have a life filled with joy. Remind yourself that you are connected with the divine creator who has an unlimited number of resources, and you lack nothing. Also, stay away from negative people. Their comments can set you back, so take care of yourself and protect your peace of mind.

"Discounting and or lowering your standards will take you off the path of achieving your goals and put you in a state of apathy."

CHAPTER 6

YOUR SOURCE HAS UNLIMITED RESOURCES

"THERE IS A SUPPLY FOR EVERY DEMAND."
FLORENCE SCOVEL SHINN

I have a teenage daughter, a freshman in high school, who shows me her nails every other week. She would say, "Dad, look at my nails. I really need to get my nails done." She would show me how her nails have been growing and constantly request that she get her nails done to manicure their appearance. There were also moments when she no longer favored the color of her nails and because of this, she had another reason to request getting her nails done.

Following a week of my daughter asking me to get her nails done, my wife and I scheduled family pictures for Christmas. As we were preparing for the pictures, picking outfits, and discussing themes for our photos, my daughter again reminded me, "Dad, I need my nails done." I took a look at her nails and said, "They look fine. No one will even notice the things you are pointing out." She rolled her eyes in disagreement and held firm to her belief that she needed a manicure.

On the Friday before our scheduled pictures and prior to me picking up my daughter from school, she called me. She said, "Hey, Dad, I want to let you know that I have scheduled an appointment to get my nails done today at 6:00pm. The nail shop is around the corner from our house, so you can drop me off on our way home." At this point, I was surprised and said, "Oh ok." When I picked her up from school, I said, "It's fine that you took it upon yourself to schedule your appointment, but do you have any money to pay for your manicure?" After I asked this question, she looked at me with a grin and said, "No, I don't have any money." I said, "How could you schedule an appointment for a manicure, and you don't have any money?" Her response was that she thought that I would pay for it. Consequently, I did drop her off at the nail shop and gave her the money she needed.

Essentially, my daughter made an appointment to receive a manicure with the faith that her father would provide the resources needed to get it done. Imagine if we all recognized that the true source of our resources is unlimited and that we don't have to give up on the things we desire just because it doesn't look like we currently have the resources to obtain them. As the opening quote from Florence Scovel Shinn says, "There is a supply for ever demand." This is another reason to never say that you cannot afford something because the truth is, there are enough resources available to obtain anything you desire. The source of your resources may not always be obvious, but if you recognize that God is your source and that His resources are unlimited, then nothing you ask for is too much for God to supply.

Consider the economic principle of supply and demand. Supply and demand in economics explain the relationship between the sellers of resources and the buyers of those resources. The principle outlines how the prices of those resources can be impacted by the supply on hand and the demand from the consumer.

For example, if someone desires the latest pair of sneakers or the newest game console and the maker of those products only has produced a limited supply. Then it is likely that if these items are strongly desired by many people, the price of these products will be increased. This is because with the shortage of supply, compared to the demand in the marketplace, people would be willing to pay premium prices to get those items. The premium price does not directly reduce demand for the product, but it is meant to provide only for those willing to pursue their demand at a higher price point. Not everyone is willing to pay the price, but this is why resale stores are so successful. People are willing to pay two to three times the original prices of a product just to have it in their possession.

This is what demand really is. Demand is the desire to have a good or service. Although the pursuit of the demand can be altered by a price increase, when people understand who the provider of their resources is, they are not moved when it costs more than expected.

Sadly, far too many people hold themselves back because they don't know their source and because of it, they give up on their desires and settle for things that are more easily achievable. The problem with taking the easy route is that when you give up on your desires and dreams, you give up on a piece of yourself in the process. This isn't the same as re-focusing goals or having better direction on what you want to do. Instead, it is considering the challenges associated with accomplishing your goals and rather than doing what is required (or paying the price) to pursue it, one takes the most convenient path without acknowledging that there is a source that can provide for all of our desires.

Oftentimes, people give up on their dreams because they become overwhelmed by the commitment required to pursue that dream. I came across a quote from Jeremy Riddle that says it best, "Every dream has a process and a price tag. Those who embrace the process and pay the price, see the fulfillment of the dream. Those who don't, just dream." Taking this thought a step further, I'd add that anything worth having is worth paying for and to never hold yourself back by a price tag because you have an unlimited source available to help you pay for anything you desire.

I didn't grow up in a rich family. My mother was a single parent who had me prior to her high school graduation. Although this was one of the most challenging circumstances for her, causing her to sacrifice so much, it never stopped her from working hard and providing the best she could for me. Upon my mother's high school graduation, she got a job working the graveyard shift at the local hospital. And though we weren't rich by American standards, we had more than enough to cover what we needed. I don't have quite the same experience as my daughter, where I took it upon myself to sign up for something, but when I was young, I was very active in sports. I started playing baseball at the age of six and football at the age of 9. Every year of playing sports, my teams required the purchase of new uniforms, and I often needed new equipment. I never thought about how these things were paid for, but I knew my mom purchased all of them. In hindsight, I now recall my mother working overtime to earn extra money to buy all the uniforms and equipment I needed to perform at the best of my abilities. I didn't notice this back then, but now I can acknowledge all the hard work she did with gratitude. She worked tirelessly to provide for everything I desired and needed. I didn't notice at the time, but her unseen efforts materialized in me having everything I needed to do the things I desired.

The truth of this point is that whether we notice or acknowledge it or not, there are spiritual forces working on our behalf. We cannot see that they are putting things in place for us to have the resources we need to do the things we desire. We just need to activate our faith to receive all that is being prepared for us.

STATEMENT OF AFFIRMATION

I am so happy and thankful, now that I know my source is unlimited. I am one with my source, and there is nothing I cannot achieve. The desires of my heart are in line with my purpose, and I have every resource needed to fulfill my purpose.

ACTION PLAN

If you have been following the action plans from prior chapters, you now have a budget that gives you a clear picture of what your resources on hand are. Now bless your budget and pray that you receive the insight needed to enhance your earnings. Many times, financial advisors tell people to look for ways to lower their expenses to create additional cash to do the things they desire. I agree with this, but I think it is equally important to look for ways to increase your income as well. Consider the opportunities on the internet and social media, like monetizing TikTok and YouTube channels or start a small business. There are so many ways to generate additional cash to fund the things not currently covered in your existing budget. Be creative and know that your source is limitless.

"God is your source and His resources are unlimited."

CHAPTER 7

VICTIMS, CONSUMERS, OR PRODUCERS

"IN TIMES OF CHANGE LEARNERS INHERIT THE EARTH; WHILE THE LEARNED FIND THEMSELVES BEAUTIFULLY EQUIPPED TO DEAL WITH A WORLD THAT NO LONGER EXISTS." ERIC HOFFER

There are three mindsets I want to highlight. These mindsets are ways that people operate that either help them accomplish their goals or hinder them from accomplishing their goals. The three are: the victim mindset, the consumer mindset, and the producer mindset.

THE VICTIM MINDSET

When someone operates with the victim mindset, they blame others, their experiences, and all sorts of external factors for their current results. If they are asked why things are the way they are, they immediately point to external factors. As a result, individuals with this mindset seek external factors to assist them in changing their situations. In essence, they are looking to be saved, helped, or rescued by someone or something. The issue with this way of thinking is that because it is a strong belief, they take no responsibility to change things in their life. They often operate by saying, "it is what it is." This statement basically means that they have no control over their situations; and in order for things to change, other external factors need to change.

The flaw in this thinking is the blatant disregard to currently living in the most opportunistic time in modern history. With the explosion of e-commerce opportunities, whether it be working from home or even starting your own business, we now have more opportunities than ever before to change things about our lives financially. Gone are the times when people were limited to just one job that barely covered the things they desired. But now, if you have a car, you can instantly become a cab service via Uber or Lyft. If you have a computer and a phone, you could instantly become a customer service representative from the comfort of your home.

The economic world is changing rapidly, and there are abundant opportunities. It's only a matter of how one prioritizes their time and their willingness to go beyond what they see around them and do what is required to create change. Arthur Ashe said it best, "Start where you are. Use what you have. Do what you can," which translates to take the steps to do what you want to do regardless of where you are and what you have. Never allow yourself to become a victim or slave to the past. This will only keep you in bondage and further from opportunities to become financially free.

My caution for someone dealing with the victim mindset, never put too much faith in things that come for free. When things are given for nothing, many times they come with a burdensome psychological price tag. For example, when things are given to you for free, you immediately feel that you must be appreciative and show gratitude. And if you don't show the desired gratitude, it can cause you to feel guilty, if it's pointed out, and even cause you to be deceived. When you pay the price for the things you desire, you avoid these traps.

I believe it is important to have gratitude for everything you have, but you should not owe gratitude to anyone for anything.

Per the Bible, you should "owe no man anything, but love." This is how people use money and gifts to manipulate others into controlling how they behave. When money is used to control behavior in relationships, it is called financial abuse. To avoid such abuse and the burden of owing anything but love, it is important to expose and remove the victim mindset.

THE CONSUMER MINDSET

When you think about the consumer, the first thing that comes to mind is the person who purchases a lot of stuff. It is the person who spends money so frequently that they don't give themselves a chance to save nor do they invest to earn more money. However, I'm not talking about that type of consumer. Such a person has his or her reason for their lack of money management skill, which might have to do with their need for fulfillment in some other area. But there is also another type of consumer mindset. The other type is the person who believes they don't have enough education to do the things they desire to gain financial freedom, so they spend most of their days getting education instead of taking action. Don't get me wrong, there is nothing wrong with education, and I believe it is wise to be informed about things you desire to pursue. However, I have seen so many cases where education has also been a stumbling block for creativity.

I have met with clients who have master's degrees, doctorates, and advanced certifications. They say they would love to start a business but don't know how. Even people with master's degrees in business have told me this. The reason they have say this is based on what they learned during their educational studies. They learned the structure of a corporation, the usual departments and their roles, and the capital required for entry into the business sector. Yet, with all that knowledge they feel unprepared to move forward.

Some have even come to me with ideas for what they desire to do. They have a business plan which needs to be completed first. They want to know if I could research the marketing cost to advertise a project that hasn't even been started. Oftentimes, my advice is to start the project first and later we will discuss the additional cost. The reason for this advice is because I have seen, time after time, that after giving all this information to a client, they go on to do nothing, saying they need to do more research in order to properly launch the project.

Many of these consumers are frustrated when they see people with less education start up a lucrative business or career. Even in cases where their career is also successful, the fact that someone with less education or a similar education from a less prestigious school can start something they have researched that seems to require more training can be frustrating. The sentiment is that someone else's success is based in luck, but the consumer worked hard for success.

Their education gives them a sense of pride that affirms the mindset that although someone may be successful in another area, it doesn't matter because they (the consumer) consider him or herself to be smarter. This mindset creates individuals who are very judgmental and block potential partnerships. Though the consumer may have professional success based on their education, they envy those who can create opportunities that free up their time while at the same time creating financial success by way of non-traditional education. This mindset pushes people away and blocks opportunities to progress beyond that which their education can provide.

THE PRODUCERS MINDSET

Producers are the people who get things done. They are not consumed by their past nor do they hoard education for the sake of being smart. Producers use their knowledge to take action to create the experience they desire. They execute on their knowledge. Producers understand that it is their responsibility to create the experience they desire. It doesn't matter where they started; all that matters is where they envision themselves in the future.

Some of the most obvious examples of producers are in the entertainment field. This is the case because entertainment is more mass communicated than other fields and professions. Producers are required to think outside the box such that they maximize their creativity to create opportunities. In addition, they must believe that they have the power to create the things they desire, which will ultimately create even more opportunities.

I believe that producers flow in creativity so freely because they stay connected to their missions. They aren't distracted by where they came from or where they are now; they are committed to the vision of where they desire to be. When you have a clear mission you seek to accomplish and are taking the steps to do so, you would be surprised how many doors open.

One of my female clients that I had for years would always talk about opening their own smoothie store. At the time, she worked at a full-time job, so she had time limitations on when she could actually open a store. She said that she had a number of recipes and wanted to make healthy smoothies for people in the community. She communicated this passion to a close circle of friends. And when those friends had parties, they would invite my client to setup a smoothie bar station for party goers to enjoy.

She would do this on the weekends for children's and adult parties. My client was consistent in her mission to provide healthy smoothies, and opportunities were beginning to open up. One day, she was approached by a colleague who said they had a vacant store front and remembered that my client mentioned wanting to open a smoothie store. My client jumped on the opportunity, opened the store, and hired the staff needed to help while she still worked at her full-time job.

What I learned from this is that when you have a clear mission/vision and are committed to doing what you can with what you got, opportunities will open up to you. This is especially true when you communicate your mission to supportive people. Potentially, the same people you are communicating your mission to and living it in front of could be the same people who help you accomplish your goals. If you recall the origin of Apple Inc., Steve Jobs was the visionary and Steve Wozniak was the computer scientist. Jobs' mission was manifested through his collaboration with Wozniak. As a result, many of you know of someone who own a product from the company they created through a focused vision and collaboration. Therefore, producers understand that the manifestation of their vision comes from their commitment to the mission and through partnerships - and not handouts.

STATEMENT OF AFFIRMATION

I am so happy and thankful that I live a blessed life filled with so many opportunities. I am thankful that the work of my hands are a blessing to my family and the world. I am so happy that I am connecting with right people who support me as I move closer towards accomplishing my goals.

ACTION PLAN

Are you believing things about your experiences, or your education that have been holding you back? What are those beliefs? For example, have you ever believed that money is the root of all evil; so, to feel holy, you don't focus on maximizing your earnings? Or have you ever felt that money would change you or the people around you so you decide to act "broke" if you get more than the average income in your community of friends and family. Take a moment and write these beliefs down and consider how they benefit you. Do they make you feel better about yourself or make you feel smart? Oftentimes, these thoughts/beliefs are sources that make people believe they are better than others. Thus, these beliefs do not benefit in any way. Now that you know these thoughts are not beneficial, you can reject these thoughts if they ever come up and move forward to fully being the producer and creator God has called you to be.

"Manifestation of your vision comes from your commitment to the mission and through partnerships, not handouts."

CHAPTER 8

NET WORTH DOES NOT EQUAL SELF WORTH

Too often, people confuse their net worth and their self-worth. When you talk to the average person concerning finances and/or their life and the value they add, their responses can easily be impacted by their financial state. The problem is that because one's net worth is constantly changing; it can cause fluctuating feelings of self-doubt and/or depression based on where one's net worth falls at that particular moment. In moments of prosperity, one may feel happy and in moments of lack or financial hardship, one may feel sad. This is why it is important to have the proper perspective and not allow money to control how you feel about yourself. One's self-worth should not be based on how much money they have but instead on who they are as a child of God created in the image of God.

Have you ever heard of HENRY? You probably are wondering, who is HENRY? Well, HENRY is not an actual person, but a type of person. In fact, HENRY is an acronym first mentioned by Fortune magazine back in 2003, which stands for "High Earners Not Rich Yet." According to the article, HENRY is loosely described as individuals and couples earning above $100k that in turn believe because they earn such a higher-than-average income, they are rich and, as a result, create luxury lifestyle habits. In reality, this way of thinking is not limited to people earning over $100k. The problem in this is that because of the lifestyle change and new habits, it slows down long-term financial growth.

When this article was originally released, it was a bit of a look at how the American dream was being lived at the time. I would further add that not only were their lifestyles inflated but so was their self-worth because of the increase in disposable income and the things they could now afford and own.

History has shown us that people were living beyond their means based on what they felt they deserved (combined with predatory lending practices by banking institutions). And when the 2008 recession hit, it exposed that many people's self-worth was tied to their possessions as financial hardship-related suicides and depression drastically increased between 2007 to 2008.

Presently, millennials are faced with the same pressure to live luxury lifestyles powered by the influence of social media. Social media gives a glimpse into the luxury lifestyles of many celebrities and gives the impression that non-celebrities are also living the same lavash wealthy lifestyle. This makes the American Dream from 2003 look like a poor man's dream. There are many more temptations for millennials today to disregard financial strategies for building wealth to live lifestyles similar to what they see on social media. This further connects their self-worth to their ability to live such a lifestyle. Thus is the reason so many millennials are depressed by not having reached a specific level of success by a particular age per social media standards. And is the reason they act "HENRY-ISH" if they are determined enough to create some level of financial success.

Many times, when you talk to the average person about financial freedom, they mention their desire to be rich and wealthy, but most don't understand what that really means. By accounting standards, wealth is determined by one's net worth; and the calculation for net worth is assets minus total liabilities equals net worth. However, the average personal standard of wealth is solely based on income, without consideration of net worth. Because of this, many aspire for arbitrary income goals without true purpose, nor do they understand how said income would be used and or why a certain dollar amount is necessary to live their purpose. This is how the HENRY attribute creeps in as without clear direction and purpose, people are vulnerable to marketers and influences that attempt to instruct them how they should live and use their disposable income.

Personally, I understand "HENRY's" and can honestly say that I used to operate in this way. I had moments when I was frustrated with earning income that only went toward bills, and thus I maxed out credit cards to fund trips and incidental purchases that I felt I deserved. In addition, I also had moments in my life where my mood would change if I looked at my bank account and saw a low or negative balance. During these times, I preferred to have fun at whatever cost because I felt I had worked hard enough to create the moments I enjoyed.

Even when following those moments, however, I didn't enjoy the consequences of having the debt.

Currently, I still believe that life should be enjoyed at the standard one creates for oneself and if you have luxurious taste, there is nothing wrong with that. However, one should be generating enough income to effectively fund their lifestyle preferences while properly managing their money and mind in the process. I don't believe that luxurious taste and high standards create problems. I believe an unhealthy mindset connecting lifestyle preferences, purpose, and self-worth creates emotional stress, unnecessary pressure and impact decision-making skills. When people operate with this unhealthy mindset, they end up depressed, stressed and make bad choices, pertaining to debt and or how they choose to earn income.

Nevertheless, when I encounter people in this state, I encourage them to consider that with a change of mindset, they have the potential to increase their income to make room for the things they desire in their lives. They can fix the bad debt decisions made in the past and become financially free without lowering their standards or compromising their self-worth. As

I said in another chapter, I feel one should never lower their standards but should instead look for ways to increase their income to meet their standards.

At the same time, I warn people not to put too much reverence toward salaries and income without a true consideration of the purpose God has called them to fulfill. My encouragement is not to only consider a desired salary but also ask why there is a need for a specific income and what is the goal and purpose for its use. These questions are often eye opening because many times, the things people desire in life aren't as expensive as they believe.

In the book titled "The 4 Hour Workweek" by Timothy Ferris, there is a parable of an American investor who took a tropical vacation. In summary, the American investor saw a fisherman dock his boat near the beach where he was relaxing. On the boat, the investor noticed large fresh fish that he hadn't normally seen, and he was impressed by this.

The investor asked the fisherman how long it took him to catch the fish. The fisherman responded, "Only a little while." The investor asked why he didn't stay out longer to catch more, and the fisherman said he only gathered enough to feed his family. The investor asked what he did with the rest of his time; the fisherman said he played with his kids, chilled with his wife, listened to music, and sipped a little wine every evening.

The fisherman went on to say that he had a full and busy life. The investor, still impressed by the fish, told the fisherman that he could help him out and had an idea for him. The investor gave the fisherman business ideas of how he could work longer to catch fish and create a business to generate much more income than he currently was making. After the investor explained how the fisherman could create a lucrative business from the sale of the fish, the fisherman asked him, "How long with all this take?"

The investor replied about 15 to 20 years. The fisherman asked, "and then what?" The investor laughed and said, "That's the best part. When the time is right, you could sell your company and become very rich, making millions of dollars." The fisherman responded by asking, "then what?" The investor then responded by saying, "Then you retire. You could move to a tropical area. You could chill with your wife, play with your kids, listen to music, and sip wine every evening."

There are a few key points that the book makes following the story, but the point I want to stress is that many people are already living the life of their dreams; they just don't know it. It's easy to look at others and base your desires on the images they give as the standard for success. But often, the things people want most can't be bought. Additionally, people are sacrificing so much of themselves, their standards and self-worth, time with family, and many other things that money cannot buy in exchange for servitude to the lifestyle they desire to attain or maintain.

For this reason, you should not focus on income alone, especially when it comes to living a standard of life connected to the purpose that you believe God has placed in your heart. Know that regardless of where you are, you don't have to lower your standards to fit your income.

You have the option to increase your income to fit your standards. But most importantly, whether you currently have the income you desire or not, your self-worth should not be a factor of your current financial state. Never confuse financial success with internal or external value.

Don't compromise your standards for money, don't stress over money, and don't get into debt to artificially fund a lifestyle you have no intention of working to earn comfortably. If you are going to use debt or credit for any reason, I suggest using it to generate more money. Use money to make money, not just to make moments. In this way, you create the opportunities necessary to both fund your dreams and payoff your debt. If you use debt in this way, I recommend considering the financial institutions lending you money as "investors." See creditors as investors and just like they seek a return on the money they give you, seek a return on how you use that money given to you.

There are financial institutions and lenders advertising credit lines and loan programs seeking to give money away to anyone with a decent credit score and a regular paycheck. Therefore, use wisdom because money is really not hard to find. Don't become a slave to your lifestyle and set yourself back. Again, I say use money to make the money required to comfortably live the life of your dreams. Never allow the fluctuation of your financial state to dictate a change in your mental state. Develop new habits that affirm "you alone are enough" and the value you add in life and to everyone in your world is beyond any monetary amount.

STATEMENT OF AFFIRMATION

I am blessed as a child of God. God has a definite purpose for my life and I am fully equipped for it. I have standards that I live by, and I will not compromise who God created me to be for any amount of money. I am a magnet for money. Money is attracted to me, and God is working every trial out for my good.

ACTION PLAN

Balance is the key to creating the life you desire while working to earn the income required to do so. Be realistic with what you want. Answer the following questions:

What do you want out of life?
What new habits can you develop to improve your confidence?

I believe that life will provide you with the necessary resources to do all the things you truly desire. Whether your route is as an employee, entrepreneur, or a combination of both, you have the power to create the income you desire for the life you deserve. Trust God and hold onto the truth in his word from Jeremiah 29:11 that states, "For I know the plans I have for you," declares the Lord, "plans to prosper you and not to harm you, plans to give you hope and a future." Trust that your present financial state has no value for what your mental state should be. Believe that all things work together for your good, and at the end of it all you are already prosperous.

"Ones self-worth should not be based on how much money they have but instead should be based on who they are as a child of God created in the image of God."

CHAPTER 9

―――― ❧❦❦❧ ――――

GIVING, RECEIVING & GRATITUDE

"YOU MUST EACH DECIDE IN YOUR HEART HOW MUCH TO GIVE. AND DON'T GIVE RELUCTANTLY OR IN RESPONSE TO PRESSURE. FOR GOD LOVES A PERSON WHO GIVES CHEERFULLY."
BIBLE – 2 CORINTHIANS 9:7

Giving is one of the most undervalued and overlooked, yet important, processes in attracting money. You may be thinking, if my goal is to make more money, how can I do so by giving it away? Well, the act of giving is not just for others; it is for you as well. Being a giver is communicating to God that you believe there is more than enough resources for you to do what you need to do and enough to help others do the things they need. It is an act of faith and belief. And as stated previously, how you live your life now is directly related to what you believe.

The issue I have seen in the concept of giving is that many people believe the wrong things and give for the wrong reasons. If you have ever been to a Sunday church service, I'm sure you have heard a minister's message concerning tithes and offerings. Sometimes, these messages are meant to cause people to question if they are properly giving according to God's standards. The hope here is to inspire attendees to understand God's standard for giving and thus as an act of obedience they should give as commanded in scripture. Doing so is an expression that God is top priority in your life above money. However, because of miscommunication and misunderstanding during these messages, many people have become givers from a place of fear instead of faith. In addition, people are confused by thinking that they should give for the soul purpose of receiving from God because they are in need and lack. This too creates giving from a place of scarcity instead of a place of abundance.

Giving in such a manner is in contradiction to the instructions in the Bible scripture 2 Corinthians 9:7 that states, your giving should be heart felt and shouldn't be based on feeling pressured. Giving should be a peaceful and joyful experience. Anytime you feel pressured to give, it can cause you to make unwise choices in response to the pressure. For example, I have worked with many accountants for clergy who stated how they frequently received bank checks to accounts with insufficient funds. This is because people are giving from a place of lack and fear and not from a place of enough.

When people give generously from the heart, God will open up doors in their professional and personal lives to be blessed from their own actions and by others. Giving is important as it keeps the circulation of money flowing. Money should continuously flow in and out of your life. It should be a blessing to you and used as a blessing to others. Operating in this manner creates the habits of the wealthy and transforms your mindset from one of scarcity to one of prosperity.

In the continuous flow of giving, you can expect to receive. And receiving is directly connected with giving as it is your way of allowing the continuous flow of blessings one to another. Have you ever seen someone refuse to take a gift? This can occur when someone believes they don't need that gift. But refusal blocks the flow and prevents the other person from being a blessing. This is why it is important to learn to receive. There is a universal principle outlined in the Bible in the book of Proverbs chapter 11 verse 25 that states, "The generous will prosper; those who refresh others will themselves be refreshed." This further reinforces the principle of giving and receiving. Thus, it is important that in the same way you allow yourself to freely give, you open yourself to freely receive as well.

Blessings are consistently flowing in and out of your life, and the key to keeping it going when it hasn't manifested yet is by having a heart of gratitude and being thankful. My mother would always say, "be thankful for what you have and enjoy your blessings." She would use it as a reminder to stay grounded, thankful, and humble. But the truth is that you open up yourself to receive more when you have gratitude for what you already have along with gratitude for what you believe God is doing for you. Having gratitude for things not yet done prepares you for actually receiving those things.

Gratitude opens up the door for you to feel more happiness and joy. Even when you are in your most challenging seasons, having a heart of gratitude can help you to refocus your attention on your source to overcome adversity and maintain the energy needed to be consistent in giving and receiving.

Gratitude also helps you keep an open mind so you don't block any blessings based on external influences. For instance, it is easy to be grateful for food when you are hungry. But, when your belly is full or you aren't hungry, you may not have the same feelings of gratitude when you are offered a meal. The act of gratitude should be an attitude you put in place in your life and not just a reaction to moments that occur.

While at the grocery store in the checkout line, I stood behind an elderly woman. When she was paying for her groceries, the clerk informed her that her card didn't go through. She said, let me try it again. Again, her card didn't go through. She thought it was a problem with her card and was confused as to why she was having issues. I considered the fact that I wouldn't want my grandmother to be in a situation like this and suggested, "I can help. I will pay for your groceries." I handed the clerk my card and paid for her items. She was extremely grateful and said, I would love to repay you. I told her there was no need, but she insisted I meet her at her car in the parking lot when I left the store. I thought nothing of it and said, sure no problem. She left the store and I proceeded to check out.

As I was walking out of the store, the elderly woman flagged me down to come to her. She said that she didn't have any cash but was the owner of an apparel store and had an inventory of custom-made COVID masks she wanted to gift me for taking care of her grocery bill. So, I took a look at the masks and selected three to my liking, thanked her for the masks, and took them home.

When I returned home from the store, I placed the masks in a kitchen drawer, as I really didn't need the masks but wanted to take them so as not to block her gifting. Later in the evening, my wife and I were planning to go out to eat and she said she would really like to have a mask that matched her outfit. I told her about the masks I had received from the elderly woman and when she saw the masks, one of them matched her outfit perfectly. She was so thankful.

Consider this, in my story, three people were blessed because of one act of giving and multiple acts of receiving and gratitude. Had I not paid for the elderly woman's groceries; she wouldn't have offered the masks that blessed my wife with one to match her outfit for the evening out. It was a cycle of blessings that could have easily been blocked if I hadn't act on what I felt in my heart. The circulation could have been blocked a second time, if I would have refused the offer of the masks as thankfulness. It all played a part. As a result, I was blessed twice, first with the gift of the masks, and second with the added gift of joy and happiness it brought my wife.

These processes don't always happen right away, but it all starts with the practice of giving from the heart. As the Bible scripture states at the beginning of the chapter, "Each man should give as he has decided in his heart. He should not give, wishing he could keep it. Or he should not give if he feels he has to give. God loves a man who gives because he wants to give."

STATEMENT OF AFFIRMATION

————  ————

I am so happy and thankful that I have the resources to give freely from the heart. I am grateful for the opportunity to give freely because it reminds me of how much I am blessed. Every day I am open to give and receive, and I am grateful and thankful for all that I have.

ACTION PLAN

———— ————

Ask yourself the following questions: When were you inspired or encouraged? Where were you spiritually feed?

Understand that the answers to these questions could be from a number of places and not just a religious institution. You could have been inspired or encouraged by the waiter at dinner. In that case, give them an additional tip above the standard 15 to 18 percent.

You could have been inspired by a family member. In that case, give to them as an expression of your gratitude.

Or you could have been inspired by a speaker online. If so, purchase their book(s) or products and/or give to a cause they support.

My point here is to understand that giving is key to attracting more. The key to giving is doing it from a heartfelt and cheerful place, and we are most cheerful in moments when we have been inspired. Also, your giving is not limited to money. If giving money is a challenge for you right now, find other areas in your life to give freely.

Recognize moments of inspiration and give without reservation or expectation and keep the cycle going. It will eventually come back to you.

"Blessings are consistently flowing in and out of your life, and the key to keeping it going when it hasn't manifested yet is by having a heart of gratitude and being thankful."

CONCLUSION

Many people pay very close attention to their money but still seek financial advice on strategies to improve their financial health. Most don't recognize that they already know what to do, but they just choose not to do it. The choices they are making in life are not always based on a lack of knowledge but because of their mindset.

People try different strategies and still find ways to fail because of their mindset. A common quote by Francis Bacon is, "Knowledge is Power." I would take this a step further and say that it's not just what you know but it's about how you implement the things you know into your life that matters.

This is how people can live in the same city but in two different worlds. It is also why relocation doesn't change people's financial state. Although they have physically moved, their mindset is the same, which creates the same or similar experiences but with a different eye view.

Understanding this is how you can avoid making mistakes and stop creating excuses. Excuses like not having time or money, or why you can't do what's needed of you are all reasons to accept failure. The reality of manifesting success in life is like the 80/20 rule. 80 percent of what you experience is based on your mindset while 20 percent is based on technical skills. Therefore, don't waste your time paying too much attention to the 20 percent when you really should be building the 80 percent, which is your mind.

Lastly, I pray that from God's glorious, unlimited resources, God will empower you with inner strength through his Spirit to do the things you desire. God has filled you with the power of creation to create the life you deserve.

In the words of Jim Rohn, "Give what you are doing… the gift of your attention." Proper attention brings proper perspective.

Now that money blocks have been exposed are you ready to take the next steps to financial freedom?

AFFIRMATIONS

―――――― ❧❦❧ ――――――

AFFIRMATION 1 – HOW YOU LEARN ABOUT MONEY, MATTERS

I have overcome the challenges of my past, and I am positioned for greatness in the future. I possess the skills and abilities to achieve God's purpose for my future. I am committed to the actions necessary to create the life I desire. I am thankful for all I have and all the blessings to come. I am healthy, wealthy, and my life is filled with joy.

AFFIRMATION 2 – DATE YOUR MONEY

I am a great manager of my money. Money comes to me in expected and unexpected ways. I attract more money into my life by thinking of things I desire to accomplish. I have more than enough and everything I need to accomplish my goals. I have clear goals, and I will never stop trying until I have accomplished all I desire. I am healthy, wealthy, and my life is filled with joy.

AFFIRMATION 3 – FACE IT TIL' YOU MAKE IT
I am so happy and thankful now that I have the ability to create the future life I desire. I am faithful and diligent in managing everything God has called me to manage. Everyday, I do my best and I trust God for the outcome. I am healthy, wealthy, and my life is filled with joy.

AFFIRMATION 4 – WEALTH IS HEALTH
I am so happy and thankful now that my life is filled with great health. I am the master of my life and money serves me for the benefit of my health, joy and fulfilling my purpose. My health is top priority in my life, and I am so happy and thankful that I have a healthy mind, body and spirit.

AFFIRMATION 5 – MONEY BLOCKS & HOW THEY LOWER YOUR STANDARDS
I am so happy and thankful now that I have overcome my past thoughts. I have put on the mind of God, and my life is filled with abundance in every area. I am worthy of all the desires of my heart. I am wealthy and can afford anything I desire. I am healthy, wealthy, and my life is filled with joy.

AFFIRMATION 6 – YOUR SOURCE HAS UNLIMITED RESOURCES
I am so happy and thankful now that I know that my source is unlimited. I am one with my source, and there is nothing I

cannot achieve. The desires of my heart are in line with my purpose, and I have every resource needed to fulfill my purpose.

AFFIRMATION 7 – VICTIMS, CONSUMERS OR PRODUCERS
I am so happy and thankful that I live a blessed life filled with so many opportunities. I am thankful that the work of my hands are a blessing to my family and the world. I am so happy that I am connecting with right people who support me as I move closer towards accomplishing my goals.

AFFIRMATION 8 – NET WORTH DOES NOT EQUAL SELF WORTH
I am blessed as a child of God. God has a definite purpose for my life, and I am fully equipped for it. I have standards that I live by and will not compromise who God created me to be for any amount of money. I am a magnet for money. Money is attracted to me, and God is working every trial out for my good.

AFFIRMATION 9 – GIVING, RECEIVING & GRATITUDE
I am so happy and thankful that I have the resources to give freely from the heart. I am grateful for the opportunity to give freely because it reminds me of how much I am blessed. Every day, I am open to give and receive, and I am grateful and thankful for all that I have.

BUDGET TEMPLATE EXAMPLE

	MONTHLY BUDGET
BEG BANK BAL.	
Take Home Income	
Other Income	
TOTAL INCOME	-
Tithe & Offering / Donations	
Vacation Savings	
Investment Savings	
INCOME ADJUSTMENTS	
DISPOSIBLE INCOME	-
EXPENSES:	
Mortgage / Rent	
Home Owners Assoc. Fee	
Gas	
Electric	
Water	
Sewer	
Trash Pickup	
Home Alarm	
Cell Phone	
Internet & Phone	
Cable TV	
Car Insurance	
Food	
Gasoline/Oil	
Household Goods	
DEBT	
Credit Card - 1	
Car Note	
Student Loan - 1	
Other Debt	
MISCELLANEOUS	
Birthdays	
Holidays	
Grooming / Hair / Nails	
Dining Out	
Entertainment	
Clothing / Shopping	
Taxes	
Vacations	
Other Special Occassions	
TOTAL EXPENSES	-
SURPLUS/LOSS	0.00
EST. ENDING BANK BALANCE	0.00

ABOUT THE AUTHOR

Patrick Howard, MBA, is servant leader, entrepreneur, tax and accounting expert. He is known for his commitment to the highest levels of ethical, professional, and personal excellence.

Patrick is the founder of Esteemed Accounting Services LLC, an accounting firm that provides tax and accounting consulting services to small businesses and individuals. In partnership with his wife, Rainie Howard, Patrick is also the co-founder of Howard Global Enterprises, an e-commerce publishing house, consulting, and virtual executive firm that provides resources to private businesses related to e-commerce admin solutions.

Prior to creating these firms, Patrick was a former NCAA Division 1 baseball player and held leadership roles in finance, tax and accounting for companies such as Anheuser Busch, the Boeing Company, Spectrum, and Curium.

Patrick uses his past athletic experience and financial expertise as a tool to educate individuals on building character, financial literacy and developing effective decision-making skills necessary to succeed in their economic futures.

To learn more, go to www.moneylovesattention.com

Instagram @phoward.cfo
LinkedIn @PatrickHowardJr.,MBA

ARE YOU ADDICTED TO A TOXIC LOVE?

The obsession of a toxic relationship can have the same enticement as drugs or alcohol. The pattern echoes time and time again: a new significant other draws you into a new relationship that starts off loving and alluring only to develop into a hurtful or abusive cycle. A person with a healthy understanding of "true love" does not tolerate this kind of pain. He or she will move on in search of a healthier bond. It's an unhealthy view of love that rationalizes toxic behavior and makes another person cling to a relationship long after it should have ended. Like any other addiction, those hooked on toxic love have little to no control over excessive urges to text, call, manipulate or beg for love, attention and affection. They want help. They want to end the pain and recover, but it's just like trying to shake a drug habit. Get your copy at http://bit.ly/AddictedToPain

Have you been trapped in a constant cycle of toxic relationships that have you frustrated with your love life?
Do you feel fear, insecurity and anxiety that has you asking yourself "am I enough?"

You Are Enough takes readers on an incredible journey of self-understanding to explore the root causes of negative emotions that are projecting themselves into their outside relationships.

The fear of never finding true love and consistently trying to please others are major factors in engaging in toxic relationships. By addressing the fear and anxiety you feel inside, Rainie helps you discover your true self-worth, which is sure to change your life!

Get your copy at http://bit.ly/YouAreEnoughBook

HAVE YOU BEEN PRAYING FOR A HUSBAND?

It's not easy to be single, and when you have a vision of being married, it's challenging to patiently wait for the right one. It's important to understand that God has a divine purpose for your life and He wants to gift you with the right man. *When God Sent My Husband* is a single women's guide to gain wisdom on:

- How to guard your heart yet freely love
- Preparing and positioning yourself to receive love
- Building a solid foundation that captures and keeps love

In this book, Rainie Howard shares her personal story of seeking love, dating, and embracing the divine experience of God bringing her husband into her life. This is a miraculous story of God as the ultimate matchmaker. The book will encourage you to take a spiritual approach towards dating and preparing for marriage.

Get your copy at http://bit.ly/WhenGodSentMyHusband

EVER FELT STUCK OR WEIGHTED DOWN BY THE PRESSURES OF LIFE?

No matter how hard you try, you just can't get unstuck.

It's like sitting in a car, pushing down on the accelerator as hard as you can with the car never moving. You are running in the race of life, but you're getting nowhere. Doors are constantly closing, opportunities are nowhere to be found, and you can't get your breakthrough. You've tried everything, but nothing seems to work. You are in desperate need of an "Undeniable Breakthrough!" Whether you need a breakthrough in your relationship, career, finances or health, this spiritual guide will give you all the life strategies needed to experience the blessings of an undeniable breakthrough.

Get your copy at http://bit.ly/UndeniableBreakthrough

Did you know that anxiety, depression, and fear stem from emotional experiences you keep tucked within your heart?

Often, people who struggle with anxiety, depression, worry, and fear are left with a sense of hopelessness. They become entangled in a battle with their own emotions, giving way to  confusion, stress, and even panic attacks. As isolation sets in, its whispering doubts make people believe they are alone, misunderstood, and sometimes even unloved. The good news is that you can find hope and healing in life's darkest moments. In Miracles In Your Mouth, you will learn the spiritual strategy to heal, renew, and transform your life. God wants to unleash His power, protection, and prosperity upon you. Will you accept it? Bestselling author, Rainie Howard, shares the mysteries of covenant prayer, powerful affirmations, and divine declarations to strengthen your mind, heal your emotions, and renew your spirit.

Get your copy at www.MiraclesInYourMouth.co

www.ingramcontent.com/pod-product-compliance
Lightning Source LLC
Chambersburg PA
CBHW070921080526
44589CB00013B/1389